Overcoming the Me Attitudes

Overcoming the Me Attitudes

Stephen Davey

ALWAYS 1ST

It's About Me!

Overcoming the Me Attitudes

Author: Stephen Davey
Editor: Lalanne Barber
Cover Design and Body Layout: Shannon Brown, Advance Graphics (www.advancegraphics.us)
Cover Illustration: Dana Thompson

Contents

Chapter One

Blessed Are the Beggars

Matthew 5:1-3

Happiness Is . . .

The magazine *Psychology Today* sent a survey to 52,000 of their subscribers, asking them to respond by telling how they found happiness or how they *believed* they would find happiness. Responses flooded in from all over the country.

Those replying from the poorer end of the economic scale dreamed of winning the lottery. This actually was the favored fantasy. Many respondents equated happiness with a winning lottery ticket.

Those people really need to take a closer look into the lives of lottery winners. I read of one individual who won nearly eight million dollars in the Pennsylvania lottery. Within a year his wife left him, winning alimony and child support that would eventually cost him about a million dollars; his landlady sued him for 30% of the winnings and won in court; his own brother and sister-in-law were indicted and imprisoned for trying to hire someone to kill him in an attempt to get his money.

Now there is one *happy* man!

Respondents to the magazine survey who were in the *wealthy* category complained that they did not have *enough* money to be truly happy. In fact, most of them complained of boredom.

Answers poured in from different geographical regions of the country as well. You might expect those living in Florida to be happier than those living in North Dakota, but that wasn't the case at all.

In the final summary, people *everywhere* were mixed up, tired, bored, angry, disillusioned, and confused. In fact, one man wrote, "I have listed below the reason I *think* I've found happiness . . . please confirm if I have."

Frankly, it didn't matter who they were, how much money they made, or where they lived—they all wanted something more or something less/something different or something else!

That's what we call the "greener grass" myth which causes every honest person to admit to wondering if there is something out there in life that will bring lasting satisfaction.

William Barclay wrote, ". . . that is human happiness; it is something that is dependent on the chances and changes of life—something life might give, but that life might also [take away].[1]

So true! In reality, the word *happiness* betrays this same truth. *Happiness* has the middle-English root *hap*, which is also found in the word *happening*.

In other words, happiness depends on what happens! We are happy if certain things happen to us; if they do *not* happen, then our happiness vanishes like a mist.

I think it is ironic that the middle letter in the English word *happiness* is the letter *i* —and rightly so.

To most people, the state of being happy revolves around *I, me* and *my*:

- What's going to happen to *me*?
- What's going to happen to *my* family—*my* health?
- What am *I* getting out of *my* job?
- What's going to happen to *my* life's savings?
- What's going to happen to *my* plans—*my* dreams?

Happiness, to the human heart, is all about *me* and *mine*.

This means, then, that *we* are the greatest obstacle blocking the way to true, genuine, blessed living.

I find it fascinating that Jesus Christ's first sermon recorded in Scripture, *The Sermon on the Mount*, identifies true, abiding happiness and how to discover it.

The Beatitudes "Supreme Happiness"

In this Sermon on the Mount, found in Matthew 5, nine times in nine verses Jesus Christ will use the word *happiness*. It is translated *blessed*, from *makarios* (μακαριος), the Greek word that means *fortunate*, *blessed*, or *happy*.[2]

Jesus Christ is going to turn it all upside down. He is going to "blow their minds."

Just look through the first few statements Jesus makes about happiness in this chapter:

- verse 3: *Blessed are the poor in spirit . . .*
- verse 4: *Blessed are those who mourn . . .*
- verse 10: *Blessed are those who are persecuted . . .*

You're thinking, "You've got to be kidding! These people sound like a bunch of losers—not winners."

And when Jesus finished these sayings, the crowds were astonished at His teaching . . . (Matthew 7:28).

There is little wonder that this was the result when Jesus finished preaching.

The people were amazed [from the Greek word *ekpleso* (εκπλησσω)]—they were beside themselves. The crowds were astounded by His teaching. Why?[3]

Matthew 7:29 explains:

. . . for He was teaching them as one who had authority, and not as their scribes.

The scribes quoted from tradition, quoted other scribes, and expounded on the words of famous rabbis and history.

Jesus Christ announces that the authority is He Himself! He says bold things to them, such as,

"You have heard that it was said . . . But I say to you . . ." (Matthew 5:18, 21-22, 27-28, 31-34, 38-39, 43-44).

Furthermore, Jesus calls God His own Father and tells everyone what God thinks and how God actually feels about certain things *(Matthew 6:14-15; 7:10-11).*

Not only that, but Jesus refers to Himself as the final Judge who actually will determine who gets into heaven *(Matthew 7:21).*

It's no surprise that the crowd was dumbfounded!

But this was yet to come. Arresting the attention of the crowd at the very beginning of this sermon was the fact that Jesus claimed to know how to find that one elusive element of life that mankind has been chasing throughout all human history: true, lasting, genuine *happiness.*

Pursuing Happiness

We in America claim to know all about the pursuit of happiness. Benjamin Franklin made this insightful comment about our own Constitution that guarantees everyone "Life, Liberty and the pursuit of Happiness." He wrote, "Please note that the Constitution only gives a people the right to *pursue* happiness; you have to catch it yourself."[4]

The trouble is that sometimes we *think* we've caught happiness by the collar. But over time, it doesn't measure up.

In New York City there are at least eight million cats ... and counting. The city is basically concrete and steel, so when those who live there have a pet that dies, they can't just go out into the back yard and bury it. The city charges a fee of fifty dollars to remove the carcass.

One rather enterprising woman thought, *I can render a service to people in the city and save them money.* She placed this ad in the newspaper: "When your pet cat dies, I'll take care of it for you for only $25." Since this was half the price of the city fee, phone calls began coming in. But here's how the business actually worked:

> The woman would go to the local Salvation Army Thrift Store and buy an old suitcase for two or three dollars. When someone called for her services, she went to the home and carefully placed the cat in the suitcase. She would then take a ride on the subway in the early evening—a perfect time for pickpockets and thieves—and place the suitcase near the door of the car. A thief would come by when the doors opened, steal the suitcase, and run out. She would yell, "Stop, thief!" What a surprise for the thief![5]

The truth is, the world is running after a suitcase thought to hold the key to happiness, but when opened, the contents never quite deliver what is expected.

Nearly 2,000 years ago, Jesus Christ delivered the news of *how* and *where* people can actually find genuine, lasting happiness. And just so no one would miss it, He gave several poignant descriptions of *who* the people are who find it.

Finding Happiness

Seeing the crowds, He went up on the mountain, and when He sat down, His disciples came to Him. And He opened His mouth and taught them . . . (Matthew 5:1-2).

The traditional posture of a rabbi while he was teaching was to be seated. When he sat and taught, it was official business.

Even to this day, we refer to a professor occupying a *chair*; in the academic world, a *chair* is endowed for the teaching of some aspect of learning. We understand that the *chairman* is the official spokesperson of a board or a committee.

The phrase "he opened His mouth" is a Greek expression used to describe serious, weighty statements.[6]

These statements by Jesus are called "Beatitudes" in most Bible outlines. The word plainly means *supreme happiness*.

Jesus Christ will deliver the surprising news that true happiness has nothing to do with an *external* situation—it has everything to do with an *internal* spirit.

What we discover in these beatitudes are the keys to overcoming *me*-attitudes—those which stand in the way of genuine happiness.

Happy Are the Poor in Spirit

The reason Christ's first statement stunned the minds of the crowd and rocked their world is in Matthew 5:3, where Jesus said,

Blessed are the poor in spirit, for theirs is the kingdom of heaven.

These people had been hearing from their rabbis for generations, "Blessed are the *perfect* in spirit, for theirs is the kingdom of heaven."

But Christ was saying, in effect, "Blessed are those who recognize they are *not* perfect in spirit."

Now just what does "poor in spirit" mean?

The word translated *poor* is *ptochos*, which is extremely descriptive of someone facing total bankruptcy.

In the days of Christ this word would be used for a person who was "as poor as a beggar."[7]

It referred to a kind of poverty so deep that the person needed help to just survive. Literally, he would be entirely dependent upon someone else for everything.[8]

Poverty of spirit, then, is an awareness that in ourselves there dwells no good thing *(Romans 7:18)*, and we are completely and utterly dependent upon Christ for everything.

As a result, only the spiritually bankrupt inherit the kingdom of heaven—they are the ones who entrust their eternal future to Christ alone.

Spiritual Bankruptcy

Thomas Watson, a wonderful Puritan pastor (1620–1686), wrote on this text, "This signifies those who are brought to the sense of their sins, and seeing no goodness in themselves, despair in themselves and [appeal] wholly to the mercy of God in Christ."

He went on to say, "Until we are poor in spirit we cannot receive grace, for we are swollen with self-excellency and self-sufficiency. If the hand be full of pebbles it cannot receive gold. Until we are poor in spirit, Christ is never precious. We only see our wants and never see Christ's worth."[9]

The world would say, "Happy is the man who is always right; blessed are those who have it all together."

Yet, Christ effectively says, "But I say to you, blessed are those whose hands are empty—those who recognize their spiritual bankruptcy . . . they are the ones on the road to genuine happiness."

The words *in spirit* refer to the inner man, not the body.

The inner person begs for the strength of Christ; the inner man is humble and contrite of spirit and trembles at My word *(Isaiah 66:2).* The Lord saves those who are crushed in spirit *(Psalm 34:18);* the sacrifices of God are a broken spirit; a broken and contrite heart, O God, You will not despise *(Psalm 51:17).*[10]

This is fundamentally the difference between the hypocrite and the child of God. The hypocrite will boast in what he has *externally*; a true child of God mourns what he lacks *internally*.

A hypocrite is happy because he is so good. This is the Pharisee in Luke 18:9-14, who went into the temple to pray and reminded God how *good* he was: he fasted; he tithed; he acted honorably. But the tax collector, who was also there, merely reminded God how *bad* he was and cried out like a bankrupt beggar, "God, be merciful to me, a sinner!" *(Luke 18:13b).* This humble man inherited the kingdom of heaven.

Spiritual Solvency

I often have people say to me, "Stephen, there's something wrong with me—I want to be like Christ, but I'm so unlike Him; I want to become holy, but I consistently fail to meet the mark of holiness. Can I feel this way and truly be a Christian?"

My answer usually begins with reminding them that the enemy of their soul would never make them aware of what they lack of Christ—the devil will always say you have enough of Him.

So this agony of spirit happens to be wonderful evidence of the work of Christ in your heart.

I remember reading this perspective for the first time, and, oh, how encouraging it was! It was, again, from the pen of Thomas Watson, the Puritan pastor, writing on this same text: "Christian, do you grieve that you are so bad? Do you go from moment to moment needing God's supply? Do you complain to God that you lack grace? Do you complain that you need a broken heart; a thankful heart? This is a good sign . . . you are poor in spirit and the kingdom of heaven belongs to you."[11]

Imagine Christ's promise of the kingdom of heaven: "Blessed are the poor in spirit for theirs is the kingdom of heaven." This pronouncement is such fantastic news. It's not a wish, but a reality—it's theirs! And, by the way, the pronoun is emphatic, which can be translated *theirs alone.*

Who does the kingdom belong to? It belongs only to the poor in spirit. And it is a present tense verb. It belongs to the poor in spirit . . . *now!*

That means we are not just talking about the Millennial Kingdom [the thousand-year reign of Christ] but the kingdom of heaven; it's yours *now*.

One author wrote, "There is a future Millennium in which the kingdom promises become full-blown, fully realized, but the kingdom has a present tense nuance. The reign of Christ in your life is now. His reign has a future Messianic aspect; but it has a "right now" aspect. We are, *right now*, a kingdom of priests. We are, *right now*, subjects of Jesus Christ."[12]

I like the way another author put it: "The kingdom is grace and glory—grace now . . . glory later."[13]

The truth is that even after you are saved, you never outgrow this kind of spirit.[14]

Then why do we so desperately try to get beyond our sense of total bankruptcy in spirit?

Go into the average Christian bookstore and look at what is pawned off on us. Book after book tells us how to win; how to conquer all frailties; how to rule without suffering; how to live without needs.

But have you ever seen books entitled:

- *How to Be a Nobody*
- *How to Empty Yourself of Self*
- *I've Discovered My Problem and It Was Me All Along!*
- *How to Live for Something Other Than Myself*

Warren Wiersbe put it this way: "The Beatitudes are attitudes that ought to be in the believer's life. And we will rarely read of them, or be encouraged to act like them."[15]

Surprising Pathways to Happiness

Three passages where this word *makarios*, or *blessed*, appears point the way to unexpected pathways that bring happiness.

1. Happiness is found through *commitment* when the will of God is confusing.

The angel came to Mary, a confused teenage girl. Mary was no super saint, but rather, someone who submitted to the confusing will of God.

Nevertheless, in her declaration of faith, Mary said, in Luke 1:48*b*,

> . . . *from now on all generations will call me blessed.*

That word *blessed* is the same word used by Christ in His beatitude. Mary was indeed happy—totally dependent on God.

We might be tempted to say, "Sure, Mary was happy— she should be; she bore the Messiah."

Yet, look at her life. Mary was on the run, having had one angelic warning after another. Later in life she, along with Joseph's and her other children, became confused about the Lord's identity and purpose. In fact, on one occasion she and her grown children came to take Christ away privately because they thought He had lost His mind *(Mark 3:21).*

After the resurrection though, she and Christ's half-brothers understood and believed the truth of His claims, as we are told in Acts 1:14.

So, if you are under the impression that happiness only occurs in the lives of those who clearly understand what God is doing with them—think again.

Imagine that for most of Mary's life she never lived down the accusation of fornication *(John 8:41)*. Still, she was *committed* to the will of God even when it didn't seem to make much sense and found, through dependency on God, true happiness.

This route to happiness is *commitment* to Christ, even when His will is confusing.

2. Happiness is found through *persistence* when the will of God is painful.

James writes,

Behold, we consider those blessed [*makarios* or supremely happy] *who remained steadfast* . . . (James 5:11).

The context of this paragraph in James deals with happiness in, of all things, suffering.

John Calvin's sermon on this text reminded his listeners that the world would say a happy person is one who is *free* of pain. But Christ says a happy person is one who persists in following God in spite of pain.[16]

A large part of the reason for this is because that person who persists through pain is one who develops total and utter dependency on Christ, and in Him finds true satisfaction. In reality, circumstances may not change—but the believer does.

So we find another course to happiness is *persistence* in following Christ, even when His will is painful.

3. Happiness is found through *obedience* when the will of God is obvious.

Revelation 1:3 says, and I paraphrase,

Blessed are all those who read and hear and obey the words of this prophecy—those who keep what is written in it.

You may say, "Okay, if I obey, I'll be blessed—I get it." But do you really get the *whole* concept? What about those not-so-obvious directives from God? You'll find examples of those who obeyed God's commands without seeing or knowing the end result in Hebrews 11:

- *By faith Noah, being warned by God about things not yet seen, in reverence prepared an ark for the salvation of his household . . .*
- *By faith Abraham, when he was called, obeyed by going out to a place which he was to receive for an inheritance . . .*
- *By faith Abraham, when he was tested, offered up Isaac . . .*
- *By faith he [Moses] left Egypt, not fearing the wrath of the king . . .*
- *By faith they [the Israelites] passed through the Red Sea as though they were passing through dry land . . .*
- *By faith Rahab the harlot did not perish with those who were disobedient . . .*

- *. . . Gideon, Barak, Samson, Jephthah, David and Samuel and the prophets . . .*
- *. . . others were tortured, not accepting their release, so that they might obtain a better resurrection . . .*
- *. . . and others experienced mockings and scourgings, yes, also chains and imprisonment. They were stoned . . . sawn in two . . . tempted . . . put to death with the sword . . .*
- *All these died in faith, without receiving the promises, but having seen them and having welcomed them from a distance, and having confessed that they were strangers and exiles on the earth.*
- *But as it is, they desire a better country, that is, a heavenly one. Therefore God is not ashamed to be called their God; for He has prepared a city for them.* Hebrews 11:13, 16

Commitment—when the will of God is *confusing*.
Persistence—when the will of God is *painful*.
Obedience—when the will of God is *obvious*.

These three are surprising pathways to happiness.

The Inheritance of Beggars

Joni Eareckson Tada, the quadriplegic who has impacted the lives of so many people with her testimony, wrote in a magazine article of being a speaker at a Christian women's conference. One woman said, "Joni, you always look so together, so happy in your wheelchair. I wish that I had your joy!"

Joni responded, "I don't do it. In fact, let me tell you how I woke up this morning. This is my average day: After my husband Ken leaves for work at 6 a.m., I am alone until I hear the front door open at 7:00 a.m. That is when a friend arrives to get me up. While I listen to her make coffee, I pray, 'Lord, my friend will soon give me a bath, get me dressed, sit me up in my chair, brush my hair and teeth, and send me out the door. I don't have the strength to face this routine one more time. I have no resources. I don't have a smile to take into this day. But You do. May I have Yours?' So . . . whatever joy you see today was hard-won this morning. [And in reality, it is only what I begged from God today.]"[17]

This is why beggars are the truly happy ones. They have abandoned themselves to the all-sufficient resources of God's grace.

Blessed are the [bankrupt beggars] . . .

Oh, and don't forget—they have also inherited the kingdom of heaven!

Chapter Two

Blessed Are the Brokenhearted

Matthew 5:4

The Illusion of Happiness

Some time ago I read about an airline pilot who was flying a commercial plane over a valley with a beautiful river running through it. He was peering out the window so intently that his co-pilot asked, "What are you looking at?"

He replied, "Do you see that river down there? I used to live in one of those homes by the water. As a little boy, I sat on a log beside it and fished. Every time an airplane flew over, I would look up and wish I was flying. Now, every time I fly over this area, I look down and wish I was fishing."

During the days of Christ, the Greek island of Cyprus was one of the favorite places for personal retreats. In our day and time, it is considered a resort island where the rich-and-famous moor their yachts and play in the sun.

The island was called "the *makarios* island," or "the happy island." The reason this name was used was because it was believed that those who lived on the island of Cyprus had *everything* necessary for happiness: natural resources, fresh water, fruit trees, wildlife, and beautiful flowers everywhere.

The island was essentially self-contained—those who lived there would not have to go anywhere else to find what they needed.

Cyprus was *the* place to live. In other words, if you could live there, happiness was guaranteed.

The Greeks just naturally assumed that if they could live where they never needed anything or anyone, and where everything to sustain life was readily at their fingertips, they would be truly happy.

Eventually, everyone recognizes that this definition of happiness is flawed. No matter where we live, we would like to live somewhere else—or at least have another closet; or maybe a hundred more square feet; or a back deck; or a bigger yard. No matter what vehicle we drive, we would like to drive something else; no matter where we work, we would like to work somewhere else—for a nicer boss and a few more vacation days . . . if we had all that, and more, we'd be truly happy.

Did it occur to you that this kind of happiness is all about *me, my,* and *mine*; this syndrome could aptly be called the *Me*-attitudes.

Me-Attitudes vs. Be-Attitudes

In Matthew 5, Jesus Christ comes along and turns this thinking upside down. He delivers the stunning news that happy people are actually bankrupted, unappreciated, persecuted, reviled, needy, weeping, downtrodden, confessing people.

The truth is, that which serves as the structure of our lives—pleasure-madness, amusement and entertainment, thrill-seeking, time, energy, money, career—are all expressions of our fallen flesh in concert with the world's blindness to the very thing Jesus Christ said will bring true, genuine satisfaction.[1]

In Matthew 5:3, Jesus has already stated that it is not the well-connected and spiritually-altogether who find happiness, but the spiritually bankrupt who are blessed: *"Happy are the beggars."*

Now He adds the brokenhearted to that list:

Blessed are those who mourn, for they shall be comforted (Matthew 5:4).

This is a new approach—another uncomfortable, upside-down revelation of true happiness.

Happy Are Those Who Mourn

There are actually nine different verbs in the Greek language that express the idea of grief and sorrow, which is a good indication that God fully expects humanity to experience heartache and distress.

Paul tells us that all of fallen creation is literally groaning in pain and awaiting final redemption *(Romans 8:22)*.

Christ Himself was called the "Man of Sorrows"— literally, a man of pains and thoroughly acquainted with grief *(Isaiah 53:3)*.

Biblical Mourning

The Bible speaks of many kinds of mourning, or sorrow.

1. Tears that flow from sorrow and loss

Abraham grieved over the *loss of his wife*. In Genesis 23:2

> *. . . Abraham went in to mourn for Sarah and to weep for her.*

Those who think it is unspiritual to lament the death of a loved one need to take note of this giant of the faith.

They also may have overlooked the example of our Lord who shed tears *at the gravesite* of Lazarus. He openly wept, revealing to all His love-motivated grief *(John 11:35)*.

The strongest, most spiritually-minded Man to ever walk the planet shed tears over loss. He, above all, fully understood the sting of death and the sorrow surrounding mortality and the grave.

2. Tears of godly longing

David longed for *an intimate walk* with God and felt deep grief over the lack of communion with Him. He wrote in Psalm 42,

As the deer pants for flowing streams, so pants my soul for you, O God. My soul thirsts for God . . . My tears have been my food day and night . . . (Psalm 42:1-3).

There were the tears of Paul, longing for the *growth* and *protection* of the Ephesian church *(Acts 20:31).*

3. Tears that accompany normal living

Timothy shed tears of *discouragement* and Paul told him,

. . . I remember you constantly . . . As I remember your tears . . . (II Timothy 1:3*b*-4*a*).

A father with a sick child came to Christ, crying tears of *agony* for his child *(Mark 9:24).*

There were the tears of *gratitude* and *devotion* from a woman who literally washed the feet of Jesus with her tears *(Luke 7:38).*

There were tears while praying for *healing from sickness*, when Hezekiah was told by the prophet that God said,

. . . I have heard your prayer; I have seen your tears . . . I will heal you . . . (II Kings 20:5*b*).

Esther cried tears of *pleading* before the king, asking him to change the edict that would annihilate the Jewish people *(Esther 8:3).*

Job, when *suffering*, said,

. . . my eye pours out tears to God (Job 16:20*b*).

Those who suffered *injustice* shed the tears of the oppressed *(Ecclesiastes 4:1).*

Paul shed tears of *anguish* over the church in Corinth, telling them,

> [Even as I am writing you I am in] *anguish of heart and with many tears* . . . (II Corinthians 2:4).

And this is just the beginning!

The truth is: growing older in Christ does not mean we will cry less; it might mean we will cry *more.* Undoubtedly, spiritual maturity redefines the things that make us cry.

Warren Wiersbe records in his commentary the story of a terrible train accident that killed a number of passengers. In one of the train cars was a mother, still holding a little child in her lap. The mother was dead but the child was unharmed. When the rescuers took the child away from her mother, the little girl laughed and played. The rescue worker noticed that her candy was dirty and gently took it from her; only then did she begin to cry. She did not know anything about death, but she knew about candy.[2]

That which grieves our hearts and causes us to weep and mourn at the age of fifty should be different from the cause of crying at the age of five.

Unbiblical Mourning

Still, many people at fifty are crying over *candy*—their "toys"; not having their own way; a plunge in the stock market; the loss of a promotion.

They don't weep over an estranged marriage; a bungled family relationship; the loss of integrity. They are mourning for the wrong reasons.

The Bible records several examples:

1. Diabolical mourning

This is the mourning of a man who cannot satisfy his impure *lusting after sin*. He grieves that he lacks money and opportunity to sin even more.

While in high school, I worked at the toll booths in Portsmouth, Virginia, collecting tolls from motorists who were driving over the bridge into downtown Norfolk. One night one of the older guys said to me, "Look over the bridge at that huge waterfront hotel. Do you see all those windows? Do you realize how many people in those rooms right now are doing all kinds of [wicked] stuff? And I've gotta be here working tonight. Man, I wish I were over there!"

This guy was literally grieving that he had to work and was not in the act of sin at that moment in some hotel room.

Thomas Watson, the Puritan, wrote, "This is the grieving of the devil, whose greatest torture is that he can be no more wicked.[3]

This is Ahab mourning [*coveting*] Naboth's vineyard. I Kings 21:4 records, if you can imagine this,

> . . . [the king] *lay down on his bed and turned away his face and would eat no food.*

King Ahab was literally *pouting* because he could not get his way! Pouting turned to murder as his wife Jezebel killed Naboth on trumped-up charges. She then gave Ahab the vineyard, and immediately his spirits lifted.

By the way, this is a necessary warning to parents who allow a child to get his way with tears and anger and pouting at the grocery store or the clothing store. Do not reward self-centered tears. That is sinful mourning and the child may never grow out of it!

2. Deceitful mourning

These are crocodile tears . . . it's all for show. This is the masquerade of sorrow used only to garner *pity* and *sympathy*, or even *support*.

These are the Pharisees in Christ's day who rubbed ashes onto their cheeks to make their faces look gaunt with fasting. Jesus preached later in this message in Matthew 6:16,

> . . . *do not look gloomy like the hypocrites, for they disfigure their faces that their fasting may be seen by others.* . . .

These are the people who are always putting themselves down, hoping to hear people tell them how wonderful they really are instead. This kind of "mourning" is really a ploy to garner pity and stoke their pride.

There is nothing spiritual about gloom and despair. Jesus did not say, "Blessed are the *gloomy* Christians."

Charles Spurgeon, the nineteenth century pastor in London, once remarked that some preachers he knew appeared to have their neckties twisted around their souls.[4]

3. Depressed mourning

This is the unhealthy, imbalanced *grief* that robs the soul of hope.

This is Judas, who was filled with this sense of despair, knowing he had sinned. He admitted as much to the chief priests in Matthew 27:4, saying,

. . . I have sinned by betraying innocent blood . . .

However, the text then adds in Matthew 27:5*b* that

. . . he went and hanged himself.

Judas, effectively, drowned himself in his despair.

Paul wrote to the Corinthians of this kind of *hopeless* despair:

For godly grief produces a repentance that leads to salvation without regret, whereas worldly grief produces death (II Corinthians 7:10).

It is no surprise that the highest level of suicide among all professional occupations is within the field of psychology. Why? Because they have studied the human condition and seen and heard the depravity of the human heart. Without Christ, there is no answer—no *hope,* no cleansing cure. Without Christ, why bother?!

Comfort, Strength, and Courage for Mourners

There is a progression in these Beatitudes. Once we discover the bankruptcy of our heart in Matthew 5:3, we are led to mourn over our sin in Matthew 5:4, which ultimately brings the comfort of burdens lifted and sins forgiven by Christ.

In this pathway to happiness, Jesus is talking about healthy mourning—weeping over sin.

He uses the strongest Greek word for mourning. He is speaking of that same deep level of grief we feel when we mourn over the loss of loved ones.

In this context, Jesus is telling us that mourners discover true happiness because they are the only ones who are grieving over their sins and their sinfulness. And in so doing, these are the ones who come to the Savior for forgiveness.

The first time you mourned over your sin and confessed to Jesus Christ, your status was changed forever—from sinner to redeemed saint.

Cleansing Words

I John 1:7 tells us that as we confess our sins,

. . . the blood of Jesus . . . cleanses us . . .

This word is *katharizei*, from which we get our word *catharsis*—cleansing.

This verb indicates that God does more than forgive; He *erases the stain of sin*. Even more encouraging is the fact that the tense is present active—denoting a continual process.[5]

The blood of Christ did not just cleanse us in the past, relative to our status; it cleanses us in our ongoing, daily experience. The blood of Christ *continually* cleanses us from all sin. Even today, the blood of Christ is washing you from every stain.

The hymn writer put it this way:

> *There is a fountain filled with blood*
> *Drawn from Emmanuel's veins;*
> *And sinners plunged beneath that flood*
> *Lose all their guilty stains.*
> *Dear dying Lamb, Thy precious blood*
> *Shall never lose its power*
> *Till all the ransomed church of God*
> *Be saved, to sin no more.*[6]

What great truth this is! Until our final redemption and glorification, the fountain is *never* turned off.

Confident Words

I remember witnessing to a Hindu some time ago; he was cheerful and kind, polite and well-mannered. Although I knew the basic tenets of his religion, I still asked him questions about what he believed.

When I told him that the difference between Christianity and Hinduism could best be summed up by the fact that he was *hoping* to have his sins forgiven and I *knew* that my God had forgiven my sins, his head dropped and his face became pained and saddened. He admitted that his religion could never provide that kind of confidence.

Jesus Christ said, "Do you want to know true happiness? Then it is not about you—because all you can do is sin. Just bring your sin to Me—I *can* and *will* forgive you!"

Comforting Words

Jesus Christ declares in Matthew 5:4:

"Those who mourn over their sin will receive comfort."

By the way, mourners are not happy because they are mourning . . . [they] are happy because they are forgiven. Happiness does not come from mourning; it comes from God's response to it—which is comfort.[7]

The word for *comfort* is the same word which forms the ministry of the Holy Spirit, who is called our *Comforter.* The root word signifies our infusion of strength and courage from Him.

Strengthening Words

This is more than sympathizing. *To sympathize* means *to feel with,* but *to comfort* means *to give strength and infuse courage into another."*[8]

When we bring our sinful hearts and hands to God and mourn over our sin, He not only forgives us, He infuses us with enough strength to carry on.

Jesus Christ did not say in Matthew 5:4,

Blessed are those who mourn—period!

No, He said,

Blessed are those who mourn, for they shall be comforted.

The verb tenses here in this text denote continuous action. We continuously confess our sin and God continuously infuses us with strength.

Martin Luther, the Reformer, wrote in his 95 Theses [the statements which ignited a future Reformation]: "Our entire life is a continuous act of repentance and contrition." It was through the comfort of sins forgiven and his justification by faith that Luther found the strength and courage to take his stand.

It is no wonder that the enemy wants us to do everything *except* keep an eye on our sinful hearts and our desperate, daily need for Christ. Because he knows that when we do come to Christ to confess, He responds with *comfort* and *strength* and *courage*.

Five Sources of Comfort

1. We are comforted by God the Father.

II Corinthians 1:3 says that

. . . God [is] *. . . the God of all comfort.*

There are times when we all need a father's comfort.

There is a vivid memory etched in my mind—a day when one of my sons *hugged* a tree in our back yard. The tree had a "ladder" of nails driven into it, and he used them for climbing. I was about fifty yards away, watching and admiring the athletic prowess of my son, as he hung from the first branch eight feet from the ground. But his foot slipped off the nail and I saw his body swivel around to the other side of the tree.

As he held on to the trunk with one arm and wrapped a leg around the tree, he yelled for help. I began moving quickly toward the tree, but he didn't wait for me to arrive.

Overcoming the Me Attitudes

He hadn't yet discovered that sometimes it hurts more to let go than to hang on, so—he released his hold on the branch. He slid down the trunk and skinned himself on the head of every nail protruding from the tree. He was painfully scraped from his waist to his chest.

He hit the ground, immediately bounded up, and came running. His feet were moving so fast that he even fell once as he ran. When he reached me, he leapt into my arms and began to wail. I just held him and hugged him, because I knew he was experiencing more pain than he had ever felt before. I did what comes naturally to any parent witnessing his child in pain . . . I comforted him.

Do we really think God will do any less for His children? No, you will find in Him a perfect Father who will provide you with all comfort.

2. We are comforted by God's Word.

Paul wrote in Romans 15, verses 4 and 13 that

. . . through the encouragement of the Scriptures we . . . have hope. Now may the God of hope fill you with all joy and peace in believing, that you may abound in hope by the power of the Holy Spirit.

3. We are comforted by God's Spirit.

Christ promised His disciples that God the Father would

. . . give you another Comforter . . . (John 14:16).

This Comforter would be a permanent infuser of hope, comfort, strength, and courage.

4. **We are comforted by God's people.**

    II Corinthians 1:4 says that God

    . . . comforts us . . . that we may be able to comfort those who are in any affliction, with the comfort with which we ourselves are comforted by God.

    In other words, we are in this *together*.

5. **We are comforted by God's promise.**

    Remember, God has not promised to completely alleviate the conditions that cause mourning until that day, when

    He will wipe away every tear from [our] *eyes . . .* (Revelation 21:4).

    Do you know one of the distinctive emotional differences between people in heaven and people in hell?

    In heaven all tears of suffering and sorrow and tears of mourning over sin will be wiped away. On the other hand, we are told that in hell there will be

    . . . weeping and gnashing of teeth [forever] (Matthew 8:12).

    Those in hell will be weeping never-ending tears and will never, ever be able to stop.

Happy Tears

So Jesus is effectively saying in this passage, "Do you know who the truly happy people are? Happy people are the ones who bring their sins to Me; they are the moment-by-moment confessors."

Now we can better understand Matthew 5:4:

Blessed are the brokenhearted, for they shall be comforted.

Not only now—but *forever*.

Chapter Three

Happy Are the Helpless and Hungry

Matthew 5:5-6

J esus Christ is in the process of giving the believer the formula for genuine happiness. And it is upside down from conventional thinking.

In fact, throughout His Sermon on the Mount, beginning in Matthew 5, He will reverse the wisdom of the world:

- Those who come in *last* are *first*;
- *Giving* is really *receiving*;
- *Dying* is actually *living*;
- *Losing* is truly *finding*;
- The *least* is, in reality, the *greatest*;
- Being *poor* is becoming *rich*;
- *Weakness* is *strength*;
- *Serving* is actually *ruling*.[1]

"Blessed are they," Christ will say nine times as His radical sermon begins. And He began with these shocking statements:

Happy are the beggars . . . Blessed are the brokenhearted . . . [paraphrased] (Matthew 5:3-4).

Now our Lord delivers another surprising step toward true happiness.

Happy Are the Helpless

Blessed are the meek, for they shall inherit the earth (Matthew 5:4).

"You've gotta be kidding. The meek are doormats—and doormats are to be stepped on!"

Matthew Henry, the Puritan pastor of the late 1600s, wrote that modern audiences recoil at this path to happiness. His words:

> "Common sense dictates that people who are meek will suffer insult and abuse, unable even to find some small corner where they can draw their breath—they are lambs among a pack of wolves; we know [by nature] that we must hunt with the hounds, because to be a sheep is to risk becoming someone else's dinner."[2]

Most modern dictionaries will define the English word *meekness* along the lines of "deficient in courage," or "one who lacks spirit and backbone".[3]

My online dictionary defines it with words like *docile; overly submissive; spiritless.*

Of Doormats and Weaklings

This is like the kid on the bus who finally got fed up with having his lunch money taken away from him by the neighborhood bully. Every day the bully demanded a dollar bill, which amounted to a whopping five bucks a week. One day the harassed boy saw an ad for karate lessons and was so excited—until he found out the lessons cost five dollars a week! So, he just continued to pay the bully . . . it was a lot less work.

The opposite approach was taken by a teen in New York City. The fifteen-year-old was almost robbed by two young thugs as he was walking from the bus depot to his father's apartment in Upper Manhattan. A gun was trained on him and the demand was made that he hand over his wallet. He said, "No!"

The toughs tackled him and went for his back pocket, but he yelled and fought back until people came to help and the would-be-thieves ran away. One of his rescuers said, "They had a gun—why didn't you just give them your wallet?"

He said, "No way, my learner's permit's in there!"[4] In other words, he'd rather die than not be able to drive. That's more like it!

Let's face it, the meek do not inherit the earth—they get ground *into* the earth. The meek lose their lunch money and their driver's permits . . . and everything else.

So you might expect the Lord to say, "Do you want to be happy and on top of the world? Well then, you need to know that the powerful and well-connected inherit the earth!"

Instead, He says, "Blessed are the meek."

But . . . isn't meekness *weakness*?[5]

Actually, nothing could be farther from the truth!

The Meaning of Meekness

The Greeks used this word translated *meek,* or *praus* (πραυς), in a number of interesting ways—all shedding light on what Christ is talking about:

- **a comforting fire in a fireplace**—when controlled, fire brings warmth; when out of control, fire brings destruction.
- **a gentle breeze**—just the right amount of wind can sail a boat or cool a hot afternoon; too much wind and we call it names like Hurricane Katrina, bringing death and destruction and loss.
- **medicine**—a patient struggling with a fever could be given medicine that was *praus* [πραυς]; that is, capable of relieving the burning fever and allowing the patient to sleep.[6]

What do all these things have in common? They can be comforting and helpful if they are contained and experienced in the right amount, but too much—and they become deadly.

Meekness is not weakness. The truth is, the biblical idea for meekness is *power under control*; it is *strength contained*.

Meekness is having the ability to strike back but resisting the urge to get even.

It is the power of Jesus Christ cleansing the temple with a whip, to defend the honor of His father.

It is the silence of Christ before Pilate, unwilling to defend Himself.

It is not being *defiant* about yourself. It is not *standing up* for yourself. It is not *defending* yourself.

One author wrote, "Meekness is being *done* [finished] with *me*."[7]

Meekness is *dying* to me. It is replacing the spirit of Me-attitudes with the principle of the Beatitudes.

Notice the promise again:

. . . the meek . . . shall inherit the earth.

The word *inherit* is a future tense verb. One day future, the meek are going to rule the planet.

Now think about the fact that we do not receive an inheritance until somebody dies—right? In this case, it is *we* who die—we die to self, to our demands, to our rights, to our way, to our will.[8]

In dying to self, we find true happiness—when we are finished with ourselves. Then we are actually free to revel in the truth that one day we will fully share in the inheritance of Jesus Christ.

This is the promise of Paul to the Corinthians:

So let no one boast in men. For all things are yours, whether Paul or Apollos or Cephas or the world or life or death or the present or the future—all are yours, and you are Christ's . . . (I Corinthians 3:21-23*a*).

Your spirit can reflect happiness even when you have been stepped on and mistreated and abused and ignored. How? By recognizing that one day, because of your relationship with Jesus Christ, you will rule the world.

Imagine that—the slaves of Christ will one day rule the world. Evidently Paul thought this was a pretty exciting prospect.

A Self-Exam for Meekness

So how do we know if we are dying to self and developing meekness? Take this pop quiz:

1. When confronted with the truth, I . . .

The word *meek* appears in James 1:21, which reads,

. . . receive with meekness the implanted word . . .

When confronted by the Word of God, the response of the meek is not to defend themselves, but to submit themselves to the truth.

2. When challenged about my faith, I . . .

Peter wrote,

. . . always be ready to give a defense . . . for the hope that is in you, with meekness and [respect]*; having a good conscience . . .*

For it is better, if it is the will of God, to suffer for doing good than for doing evil (I Peter 3:15-17).

Here again is the nuance of dying to self rather than defiantly standing up for self. It appears as voluntary helplessness in the face of those who might grind us into the dirt.

And just look at who wrote those verses:

- *Out-of-control, sword-swinging, ear-chopping-off* Peter
- *Talk first/think last* Peter
- *Control-my-emotions? . . . what-fun-is-that* Peter

That's right—Peter wrote those verses! And this should give us all hope—not only in surrendering to this attitude of meekness, but in the fact that the person who wrote about that attitude was Peter. Evidently *he* had grown in meekness over the years, which means that we can, too.

3. When others are caught in sin, I . . .

What's your response to discovering sin in another person's life? Does your phone bill suddenly go up? Are you leading the pack in gathering stones for throwing? Are you making notes for the speech of your life?

Paul told us how we should respond in Galatians 6:1:

. . . if anyone is caught in any transgression, you who are spiritual . . . restore him in the spirit of meekness.

This is a warm fire; a gentle breeze; just the right dose of medicine.

Perhaps you're thinking, *I'd like to do better on the next pop quiz. How can I cultivate more meekness in myself?*

Before you write down ten ways toward becoming meeker and buy a coffee mug that says, "I'm Committed to Meekness," I have only one reminder—don't forget that meekness is a fruit of the Spirit, translated *gentleness (Galatians 5:22-23).*

We can't drum-up meekness. The Spirit of God *develops* meekness over a lifetime as we surrender to Him [think: Peter].

So let's review the pop quiz:

- How do you respond when confronted with the truth?
- How do you respond when challenged about your faith?
- How do you respond when another Christian falls into sin?

Now let's move on as our Lord brings up another distinctive of true happiness.

Happy Are the Hungry

The Lord delivered yet another stunning declaration:

Blessed are those who hunger and thirst for righteousness, for they shall be satisfied (Matthew 5:6).

In order to understand what the Lord meant, we have to answer a couple of questions. Was He referring to an *objective righteousness*—the righteousness of God imputed [credited] to our account at conversion?

It can't be, for we already *have* this righteousness as a gift of God through faith in Jesus Christ *(Romans 3:21-22).* We have been declared righteous—that is, right with God.

Okay then, is this some kind of *social righteousness* in the just treatment of the poor and oppressed?

It could be . . . however, every one of the seven occurrences of *righteousness* in this Sermon on the Mount refers to *subjective righteousness.*[9]

The Lord isn't talking about *being* right with God as much as He is talking about *living* right for God.

Simply put, hungering and thirsting after righteousness refers to a passionate longing for living a life pleasing to God. And when God is pleased, we are pleased. Paul wrote,

> . . . *it is my ambition to be pleasing to God* [paraphrased] (II Corinthians 5:9).

Our greatest happiness is found in God's happiness. Our greatest pleasure is found in bringing God pleasure. What satisfies genuine believers most is found in satisfying God.

Jonathan Edwards, who pastored in the mid-1700s, wrote,

> *The enjoyment of God is the only happiness with which our souls can be satisfied. Fathers and mothers, husbands, wives, or children, or the company of earthly friends are but shadows, but enjoyment of God is the substance.* [Family and friends] *are but scattered beams, but God is the sun. These are but streams, but God is the fountain. These are but drops, but God is the ocean.*[10]

How's Your Appetite?

The paradox of this beatitude is that we are satisfied with that which makes us hungry. We are hungry for right living and satisfied in living it, which makes us only hunger for it all the more.

This sounds like Thanksgiving dinner to me! We are stuffed—we can't eat another bite—we are satisfied beyond reasonable proportions . . . *ahem*! But a couple of hours later, what are we doing?—making a turkey sandwich!

Does this prove we're gluttons? Maybe. But more than likely it simply proves that we are *alive*!

Think about it: the deceased have no appetite . . . only the living do.

So, this is a beatitude, like all the others, for the living. And solid proof that we are alive is the fact that we are constantly hungering and feeding our hunger, and quenching our thirst—only to realize that we must have our thirst quenched all over again . . . and again.

Now, we could rewrite this beatitude in the form of a two-fold question: What exactly are you hungry for, and just how hungry are you?

Aristotle wrote of a time when one of his young students came to him and said, "Aristotle, you have wisdom that I so desire to have. How can I have it?"

Aristotle said, "You really want it?"

The young man said, "Master, I do."

Aristotle then said, "Well then, follow me."

He walked across the portico of the building, out into the courtyard, and without hesitating, waded directly into the pool of a fountain with water nearly waist-high. The young man hesitated, and then thought, *Well, he said to follow him in order to find wisdom.* So, gathering up his robe, he climbed over the edge and joined Aristotle.

When they were in the middle of the pool, Aristotle suddenly turned, grabbed the young man by the nape of the neck, pushed him under the water, and held him there. The youth thrashed his arms and kicked his legs, desperate to breathe.

At the last moment, Aristotle picked him up and carried him to the side of the pool.

The young disciple was coughing and sputtering in shock and rage, but Aristotle ignored it all until the young man stopped gasping. Aristotle then asked him, "When I held your head under water, what did you want more than anything?"

"Air, sir, *air*!" the young man cried.

His teacher then said, as he climbed out of the pool, "When you want wisdom as badly as you wanted air, you will have it."

That incident makes me ask the question, "What do you want more than anything? Do you want to please God? How badly do you hunger for His pleasure in your life?"

Frankly, a starving man doesn't want food *and* a new car. He just wants food.

A man dying of thirst doesn't want water *and* a business promotion. He just wants a drink of water. [11]

Nothing else matters to him; we don't have to add anything to the list to satisfy him after giving him food or water.

If you ask the average Christian, "Do you want to please God with your life?" the answer would probably be, "Sure —and I also want Him to give me this, and this, and this, and that."

Perhaps the average Christian isn't quite famished enough for holy living.

For those who aren't all that hungry, they may not recognize the fact that their lack of hunger and thirst for *righteousness* is their greatest obstacle to genuine *happiness*.

So praying a prayer like this is entirely legitimate: "Lord, give me a longing for You; give me a hungering after You; give me a thirst for pleasing You."

For these happy ones, God alone satisfies.

Satisfied beyond Measure

Given what we have discovered in this chapter, I have rewritten these two beatitudes which enable us to overcome the Me-attitudes:

"Blessed are those who refuse to stand up for their own rights, willingly helpless as they refuse to exercise their power, even when it means they get bruised in the stampede of life, yet happy in knowing that one day, they will rule the world with Christ."

"Happy are those whose primary appetites in life are living for God's pleasure—assured that God will satisfy them and deepen their hunger to grow and be filled, and grow even more and be filled again, over and over—until perfected in holiness one day in His presence, completed with satisfaction in heaven . . . *forever*.

Chapter Four

Happy Are the Helpful and Holy

Matthew 5:7-8

Faithful, Fruitful, Insightful

He was born in 1897 in a tiny farming community in western Pennsylvania. One night, at the age of seventeen, while walking home from his job at a tire store, he overheard a street preacher say, "If you don't know how to be saved . . . just call on God."

When he arrived at home, he did that very thing. He climbed the steps into the attic of his parents' home and called out to God for salvation.

Five years after his conversion, he took his first pastorate in West Virginia. Without any formal training [although he later would become an incredible student of the Word and teacher of Christian principles], he entered the ministry.

This was the beginning of forty faithful, fruitful years that included authoring numerous books, pastoring several churches, receiving two honorary doctorates, and heading a national magazine as editor, producing countless articles with a pen laced with a touch of sarcasm, a good measure of wit, and a load of spiritual insight.

His name was Aiden Wilson Tozer, better known as A. W. Tozer.

His books, *The Knowledge of the Holy* and *The Pursuit of God*, are now considered across denominational lines to be Christian classics.

Though loved by many, Tozer stood for the truth of the Gospel. In fact, in an era in which liberalism had swept into the mainline church in the early 1900s, he wrote, "We are not diplomats, but prophets, and our message is not a compromise—it is an ultimatum."

Tozer further challenged the average American church that had grown stale over time, when he wrote,

> *One characteristic that marks the average church today is a lack of anticipation. When Christians meet, they do not expect anything unusual to happen; consequently only the usual happens, and that usual is as predictable as the setting of the sun. . . . We need today a fresh spirit of anticipation that springs out of the promises of God as we come together with childlike faith.*

More than anything, A.W. Tozer had the ability to challenge the believer to dig into the Word of God. He wrote, "We must not select a few favorite passages to the exclusion of others. Nothing less than a whole Bible can make a whole Christian."

He compared the Bible to a wristwatch and, with a touch of sarcasm, wrote, "If God gives you a watch, are you honoring Him by asking Him what time it is or by consulting the watch?"

If you have read Tozer's books, you know that even though his most favorite books centered on theology, he had an unusual ability to challenge the Christian with the thought that believing the truth is not enough—in fact, it is dangerous unless we live it and obey it.

He once reminded an audience of this truth when he said, "The devil is a better theologian than any of us, yet he remains the devil."

Inside Out

On one occasion when A. W. Tozer was preaching on the Beatitudes, he made the comment that if we turned the eight Beatitudes inside out, they would reflect the thinking of the American culture. And he said *that* more than fifty years ago!

It is still true, is it not? Is it any surprise, then, that the American culture could be defined as anything *but* happy?

I took Tozer's suggestion and turned the Beatitudes inside out, contrasting what our world says with what Jesus Christ is saying in Matthew 5:

verse 3: *"Blessed are the poor in spirit, for theirs is the kingdom of heaven."*

- **the world:** "Happy are those who can say, 'I've got it made!'"

- **Jesus Christ:** "Happy are those who recognize they haven't got a chance."

verse 4: *"Blessed are those who mourn, for they shall be comforted."*

- **the world:** "Happy are those who never have to cry about anything."
- **Jesus Christ:** "Happy are those who never stop crying over sin."

verse 5: *"Blessed are the gentle, for they shall inherit the earth."*

- **the world:** "Happy are those who know how to climb the ladder."
- **Jesus Christ:** "Happy are those who voluntarily come in last."

verse 6: *"Blessed are those who hunger and thirst for righteousness, for they shall be satisfied."*

- **the world:** "Happy are those who stuff themselves with the things of life."
- **Jesus Christ:** "Happy are those who are starving for something beyond this life."

verse 7: *"Blessed are the merciful, for they shall receive mercy."*

- **the world:** "Blessed are those who never need help or a handout."
- **Jesus Christ:** "Blessed are those who are ready to lend a hand."

verse 8: *"Blessed are the pure in heart, for they shall see God."*

- **the world:** "Happy are those whose private perversions are never revealed."
- **Jesus Christ:** "Happy are those whose private purity is a daily resolution."

What an amazing contrast between the "*me*-attitudes" of the world and the *be*-attitudes of Jesus Christ!

And the Lord isn't finished with His upside-down list; He goes on to deliver this next truth.

Blessed Are the Merciful

Blessed are the merciful, for they shall receive mercy (Matthew 5:7).

Before we find out what Christ is saying, we need to understand what He is *not* saying.

- **Jesus Christ is not saying, "If you show mercy *to* others, you will receive mercy *from* others."**

If this were so, the most merciful Man to ever walk the planet would have been given mercy by the mob instead of a rugged cross.[1]

Furthermore, David, the king-elect, showed mercy on two occasions to the reigning king Saul. David could have taken the life of this cruel, vindictive king who tried to pin him to the wall with spears. For years Saul had tried to capture and murder David so he would not take the throne of Israel.

On one occasion in the middle of the night, while Saul and his men were sleeping in the open, David crept up and cut a piece from Saul's cloak—when he could have cut Saul's throat. David showed mercy and Saul only grew more vindictive.

So today, it is possible to show mercy to people who then turn their back on you, reject you, and mistreat you.

In this beatitude, the Lord is *not* saying, "If you show mercy to others, you will receive mercy in return."

- **Jesus is not saying, "If you show mercy to *others*, you will earn mercy from *God*."**

We do not earn mercy by extending mercy.[2]

Salvation from God is not merited, it is received. And receiving mercy from God is our present tense experience and our future tense experience without any "mercy requirement" on our part.

Paul told Titus,

[Christ] *saved us . . . according to His . . . mercy . . .* (Titus 3:5).

In Ephesians 2:4, Paul writes that God has saved us,

. . . being rich in mercy . . .

In other words, it is impossible to be saved without the mercy of God, and salvation is an unmerited gift from God.

You need to understand that this beatitude has more to do with your relationship with other people than with God.

I believe we could understand the Lord to be saying, "Since you are people who have and will receive the mercy of God, prove it by showing mercy to other people."

The Quality of Mercy

More than anyone else in the world, the distinctive of the believer should be mercy!

Showing mercy to others is not a condition to receiving mercy from God—it is *proof* that we have received it. Showing mercy is evidence that we have received mercy.[3]

Who better to show mercy to others than we who've received such mercy from God!

This is the thought behind the Apostle John's question to the Christian student:

> But if anyone has the world's goods and sees his brother in need, yet closes his heart against him [literally: has no mercy on him], how does God's love abide in him? (I John 3:17).

We do not earn the love of God. But how can we claim to have the love of God and yet be unloving and unmerciful to others at the same time?

Jesus Christ only adds to the incentive when he delivered this beatitude which effectively declared: "Do you want to be truly happy? Then show mercy to others."

Understand that the world of Christ did not admire mercy. The Romans admired justice, power, and physical domination. The philosophers of Christ's day actually called mercy a "disease of the soul."[4]

While in India I was so moved by the masses of people who were considered Untouchables—the lowest caste in the Hindu culture. Children ran after us wherever we went, offering cheap plastic necklaces for pennies; women carrying babies on their hips begged on the street corners as we drove by, their lives filled with unspeakable difficulty and sorrow.

Still, they received no mercy from anyone! Their religion taught that these people had been reincarnated as Untouchables because of a prior life of evil—they were getting what they *deserved*.

I met a Christian woman who was going among the Untouchables and inviting elementary-aged girls from this caste to her school. She dressed them in clean uniforms and then, in a public bathroom that she had cleaned herself, sat them in tidy rows on the scrubbed floor and taught them every week-day, giving those Untouchables hope.

What would motivate anyone to show these people mercy? Someone who had received the mercy of God herself!

And mercy is always demonstrated.

Mercy, one author wrote, is simply seeing a man without food and giving him food. Mercy is seeing people begging for love and giving them love. Mercy is seeing someone lonely and giving her company. Mercy is not in feeling their need, but in *meeting* their need.[5]

Another wise author wrote it this way, "Mercy is giving attention to those in misery."[6]

But the world doesn't buy that! In Christ's day and in ours, happiness is having people bow to our needs, not our stooping to meet theirs.

The Blessing of Mercy

The world would say, "When you are in control—when you have people at *your* mercy—that's really living."

Well, Joseph must have been really living! In Genesis 42, his brothers had come to Egypt in need of food and had bowed before his authority, not knowing he was their youngest brother whom they had sold into slavery.

Joseph now had his brothers at *his* mercy—but instead, he showed *them* mercy. This was undeniable proof of God's mercy having impacted his own heart long before their unexpected reunion in Egypt.

Do you want true happiness? Show mercy.

There is mercy in forgiveness. There is mercy when we withhold that which someone justly deserves; when we refuse to take revenge—even when that person is *at our mercy* and we can hurt them, or humiliate them, or ignore them.

Mercy is the imitation of Christ, who in His mercy saved us.

The hymn writer put it this way:

> *"By God's Word at last my sin I learned;*
> *Then I trembled at the law I'd spurned,*
> *Till my guilty soul imploring turned*
> *to Calvary."*

And what happened?

"Mercy there was great, and grace was free,
Pardon there was multiplied to me;
There my burdened soul found liberty
—at Calvary."

The one who shows mercy to the guilty reveals this truth: he has received the mercy of Christ in his past and will experience the mercy of God in his eternal future.

This is the path to true happiness.

The Absence of Mercy

Do you want to be truly *unhappy*? Be merciless! Let everyone know that those people in that group, or down the street, or in that country over there are getting what they deserve.

Joseph Stalin ["Stalin" is translated *steel*] was a former Russian premier—one of the most powerful men on the planet; he executed millions and had millions more at his mercy. And he showed *no mercy*.

This man of steel had seven bedrooms, each of which would be closed at night as tightly as a safe. He spent every night in a different bedroom for fear of being assassinated. Stalin's greatest fear was that those he led with his steel boot might show him the same lack of mercy. He even employed a full-time servant to do nothing more than monitor and protect his tea bags.

This is a happy man? His world might have thought so—he was on top of it—but here's the truth; that servant who watched the tea bags probably enjoyed his tea more than Stalin did!

Even an atheist might learn from Shakespeare that " . . . we do pray for mercy; and that same prayer doth teach us all to render the deeds of mercy."

Solomon put it this way;

The merciful man does himself good, but the cruel man does himself harm (Proverbs 11:17).

Simple enough! And Christ isn't finished yet.

Blessed Are the Pure in Heart

Mercy is an external activity but *purity* is an internal quality.

In one more packed phrase, Jesus delivers another upside-down, backward, countercultural truth on how to put away the "*Me*-attitudes" and discover the Beatitudes:

Blessed are the pure in heart, for they shall see God (Matthew 5:8).

In other words: happy are the holy—blessed are the pure in heart.

What exactly was the Lord referring to when He brought up the subject of purity?

The Scriptures speak of *positional* purity and *practical* purity.

Positional purity is the work of God *for Christians* and practical purity is the work of Christians *for God*.

Positional Purity

Positional purity is another term for justification. We are justified—declared pure and righteous by the work of God for us at salvation. That's our position of purity.

Paul wrote in Romans 3:23-24,

> . . . *for all have sinned and fall short of the glory of God, and are justified* [declared pure before God] *by His grace as a gift, through the redemption that is in Christ Jesus.*

Positional purity is the easy side of the equation because God has accomplished all the work of redemption for us.

Practical Purity

But that's not the end of the subject. When the Bible speaks about the heart, it means the center of the personality; the heart is the mind, the emotions, and the will; the heart refers then to what makes you who you are.[7]

Jesus Christ said,

> . . . *out of the abundance of the heart the mouth speaks* (Matthew 12:34b).

Solomon wrote,

> . . . *as* [a man] *thinks in his heart, so is he* (Proverbs 23:7).

Notice that the emphasis is not on our hands but our hearts. Our hands are related to mercy; our hearts are related to purity.

Practical purity is the hard part. This is our responsibility. This is who we are and what we do for God.

Personal Purity

So the happy are those who diligently and passionately desire purity: in their hearts—in their minds/thoughts—in their emotions/feelings—in their will/decision making.

Purity is from the word *katharos*, which refers to *integrity*. It is akin to the Latin word *castus*, which gives us our English word *chaste*.

Again in Matthew 5:8, the promise to the pure is

. . . they shall see God.

The tense of this verb is a future continuous tense. One author paraphrased this text to read, "Happy are those who pursue purity [in their mind, emotions, and will], because they will continually be seeing God for themselves."[8]

Warren Wiersbe said it this way, "Spiritual sight leads to spiritual insight."[9]

The best way to see the hand of God at work in your own life, the lives of others, and in the life of your world is through a heart that you continually ask God to cleanse, like David, who prayed,

Create in me a clean heart, O God . . . (Psalm 51:10).

Helen Keller was asked, "Isn't it terrible to be blind?" She responded, "Better to be blind and see with your heart, than to have two good eyes and see nothing."[10]

Blessed are those who see with their hearts . . . and those with pure [clean] hearts see the most clearly!

Walking Carefully in the Parade of the Ages

The amazing Hubble telescope, orbiting 360 miles above Earth's surface, travels at the speed of 5 miles per second, completing one full orbit every 96 minutes. It can peer into space 7 billion light years away.

Before it was launched, numerous delays caused the lens to be stored for seven years in a sterile cell in the Lockheed facility in Sunnyvale, California. The cost was a staggering eight million dollars a month.

That's a lot of rent money—one billion, four hundred seventy-two million dollars . . . and no cents!

I found it fascinating that scientists certainly understood the best way to see the heavens is through a *clean* lens.

Believers who cultivate a pure heart see the activity of the God of Heaven through a clean lens.

A. W. Tozer said it this way, "You can see God from anywhere if your [heart] is set to love and obey Him."

He wrote these convicting words: "It will cost something to walk slowly [carefully] in the parade of the ages, while excited men rush about, confusing motion with progress; but [walking slowly, carefully] will pay off in the long run."

This is another way of saying, "Don't listen to what the world says about happiness—listen to what Jesus Christ says."

Happy are the merciful . . . happy are the pure in heart.

These twin attributes go side by side down parallel paths that eventually converge at the same destination—genuine, lasting happiness.

Chapter Five

Happy Are the Harassed

Matthew 5:9-12

Say That Again . . .

A man knew his wife's birthday was coming soon, so he asked her—without trying to appear all that interested in her answer—"Honey, if you could have one wish, what would you want?"

She thought for a moment, then laughed and said, "I'd love to be eight again."

On the morning of her birthday, he woke her and off they went to a nearby Waffle House for breakfast. After a huge waffle with strawberries and whipped cream, they headed to the local theme park. What a day they had: Death Slide, Cyclone Whip, Screaming Loop, Wall of Fear, Double Ring Ferris Wheel—he made sure she got to ride *everything*!

Five hours later she staggered out of the theme park with her husband—head reeling, stomach churning. But off to McDonald's they went, where he ordered a Big Mac with fries and a thick chocolate milkshake for his birthday girl. Afterwards, he plopped down money for the latest Disney animated movie, popcorn, Pepsi, and a bag of peanut

M&Ms—topping off a day full of fabulous eight-year-old adventures.

Exhausted, she stumbled into the house late that evening with her husband and collapsed on the bed. He leaned over and softly whispered to his birthday girl, "Well now, how'd you like being eight again?"

One eye opened in surprise and she moaned, "I meant my dress size!"[1]

Poor woman . . . but he meant well!

It's one thing to think we heard someone correctly, but it's another thing to properly understand!

It is typical, is it not, for us to have to say:

- "Oh, I thought you said *that*."
- "I thought when you said it, you meant *something else*."
- "I didn't think I heard you right, so I didn't think you *meant* it."

How many husbands say, "Honey, I never heard you say that."

How many wives say, "I can't believe you didn't hear me say that."

For what it's worth, these illustrations are purely hypothetical!

What God *Really* Said

Without a doubt, everyone has an opinion of what God says on just about everything . . . certainly on what pleases Him:

- If you *do* this, God will be pleased and you will be happy.
- If you *don't* do this, God will be pleased and you will be happy.
- If you *do* this or *don't* do that, God will *not* be pleased and you will *not* be happy.

Is God really that confusing on the subject of happiness? Have we truly heard what He said?

I find it fascinating that as Jesus Christ began His first sermon, He could have said a lot of things about *a lot of things*. However, He began by clearing up the truth about happiness and how to find it.

In these brief statements, each beginning with the word *makarios* ["true, genuine, sustained happiness"], Jesus Christ radically defines a life of true happiness.

We have uncovered, in the process of studying these statements, the principle that dying to self is the first and ongoing step toward happiness.

We have discovered that the *Blessed*s [Beatitudes] are the opposites of the Me-attitudes.

Jesus Christ defined the path in Matthew 5 by thoroughly upending conventional religious wisdom. What the religious leaders and people of Christ's day *thought* God had said was totally different from what He really *meant*.

For that reason, don't misunderstand what God is saying about happiness! You might think you heard Him, but let's just make sure.

Blessed Are the Peacemakers

Blessed are the peacemakers, for they shall be called sons of God (Matthew 5:9).

"Happy are the peacemakers."

Notice that Jesus Christ does not say, "Happy are the peaceful," or "Happy are the undisturbed."

Oh, no . . . in fact, the Lord uses a compound word:

- **peace:** much the same as the Hebrew word *shalom*, which means "wholeness or well-being." When a Jew wished another person *shalom*, it was not just "have a nice day"—it was a blessing for them to have a blessed life.
- **maker:** we need to understand that this person is not a passive observer, but a negotiator of peace.[2]

By the way—take note that Christians who are peacemakers are called,

. . . sons of God.

The Lord uses the word *huios* for sons, instead of the normal word *tekna* for children. *Tekna* is the tender and affectionate term for little children. *Uios* is the term which speaks of dignity and honor.[3]

We literally bear the honor and dignity of God whenever we negotiate peace.

In the same vein, notice also that peacemakers are not given the promise of peace in return. The truth is, peacemaking can upset everything in our world. A godly person might actually stir up trouble!

Think about it—wherever the Apostle Paul went, there was either a revival or a riot!

The cross of Calvary was the greatest event of peacemaking in the history of the planet. And it cost the life of the Peacemaker.

Peacemakers do not sacrifice truth or gloss over sin. The Lord openly exposed sin and then He suffered for it! *His* death brought *us* peace![4]

Paul wrote,

Therefore, since we have been justified by faith, we have peace with God through our Lord Jesus Christ (Romans 5:1).

There was nothing cheap or easy about this peace. Paul further discloses to the Colossians:

For in [Christ] *all the fullness of God was pleased to dwell, and through Him to reconcile to Himself all things, whether on earth or in heaven, making peace by the blood of His cross* (Colossians 1:19-20).

Christ *made* peace for us. Paul uses the same root words for Christ making peace that Christ used of us being peacemakers in this Beatitude.[5]

It will cost us. We will have to die to *self.*

Peace Comes at a Price

Every time we share the gospel of Jesus Christ with someone, we are engaged in peacemaking. The world is in deep trouble at this very moment, whether realizing it or not; it is the enemy of heaven—and we beg the world to be reconciled to God.

Paul declares to the Corinthians,

Therefore, we are ambassadors for Christ, God making His appeal through us. We implore you on behalf of Christ, be reconciled to God. (II Corinthians 5:20).

I would have to admit that I've made enemies over the years because of the gospel . . . have you?

Have you ever had anyone respond to your testimony by saying, "Who do you think you are, telling me I'm a sinner?"

Now, this doesn't mean we grab people by the shirt collar and make them repeat, "I'm a dirty rotten sinner." Be that as it may, they eventually realize that is *exactly* what we are saying.

Have you ever had a door slammed in your face?

Have you ever been passed over for a promotion because you wouldn't laugh it up with your co-workers?

Have you ever been ridiculed for your faith on campus?

Standing up as a child of God may mean you stand alone.

Peace May Be Hard-Won

I have read a biography of General Douglas MacArthur, the great general of World War II— depending on which author you are reading. Japanese soldiers had dug in on dozens of islands and after the terms of surrender had been signed, many of the troops were late in receiving the news.

A few years ago the last Japanese soldier from WW II was found! For decades he had been isolated on an island—hiding out; living in fear in the jungle—not knowing that the war had ended. Equally tragic, I read that the Japanese government sent messengers to many of these islands to deliver the news that the war was over. Some of the messengers were shot and killed.

There is a parallel to this if you become a peacemaker: you may lose sleep; you may ruffle feathers; you may make enemies. You may even have snipers shoot at you. But you are willing to sacrifice *peacefulness* as you become a messenger of peace.

If you are willing to share not only in the power of His resurrection but in the fellowship of His sufferings, you are prepared to engage in delivering the news that peace with God is now available through Jesus Christ. The war can be over.

I recommend to my seminary students that they read the short biography of Robert Chapman, the pastor of a small church in nineteenth-century England. He was a man deeply respected and considered by Charles Spurgeon as the saintliest man in England.

Yet, not everyone liked Robert Chapman. A grocer once became so infuriated by Chapman's open-air preaching that he spit on him. For a number of years the grocer continued to verbally attack him. Chapman never retaliated.

On one occasion Chapman's wealthy relatives came to visit. Since Robert was a single man his entire life, they decided to cook for him and asked where groceries could be purchased. Chapman insisted they go to this particular grocer's store.

After purchasing a large amount of food, the request was made that it be delivered to the home of R. C. Chapman. The stunned grocer told the visitor that they must have come by accident to the wrong shop. "No," came the reply, "Mr. Chapman himself insisted that we come here."

When the grocer arrived with the delivery and Chapman answered the door, he broke down in tears at Chapman's graciousness and yielded his life that very afternoon to Jesus Christ.[6]

Blessed Are Those Who Are Persecuted for Righteousness' Sake

Christ actually amplifies the results of being peacemakers in the final beatitude in Matthew 5:10-12:

Blessed are those who are persecuted for righteousness' sake, for theirs is the kingdom of heaven. Blessed are you when others revile you and persecute you and utter all kinds of evil against you falsely on My account.

Rejoice and be glad, for your reward is great in heaven, for so they persecuted the prophets who were before you.

Truly happy are those who are persecuted for righteousness' sake.

Persecuted is passive in the Greek, indicating that the persecuted are giving permission; are willingly allowing themselves to be maligned, persecuted, hated, ignored—perhaps even incarcerated or killed.

Persecuted is also in the perfect tense which means that persecution is happening with continuing results.[7]

The poignant word carries the idea of being chased or pursued. We could render it *harassed*!

In these final beatitudes, Jesus Christ once again turns conventional wisdom on its head as He declares, "Happy are the harassed."

Just don't overlook the phrase He adds: "for righteousness' sake."

Punishment Isn't Persecution

When we get pulled over for running a stoplight, that is not persecution by the State. We cannot expect rewards in heaven for that.

When I was a kid, my friend and I would explore the woods near our subdivision in the summertime until it grew dark. There was an apartment complex on our way home, and the box that controlled the electricity for the entire apartment building was downstairs. We would scout around to make sure no one was outside and then pull the lever that shut off the power. Then we'd run for our lives as the entire building went dark.

The last time we ever pulled that stunt—and I do mean the *last* time—two guys [one dressed in army fatigues] happened to be standing on the balcony just above the wall where the switch was located. They heard the electrical arm slam down, saw the building grow dark, and watched two boys sprint beneath their balcony.

Putting two and two together, they shouted, "Hey, you!" As we raced away from the building, I turned and saw one of the men leap over the balcony railing, land on his feet like some superstar commando, and take off after us. If we had not outrun him, I never would have been found.

God determined that I would live to write this book!

Now, if my friend and I had been caught, we would not have been persecuted—we would have been punished.

It is important to understand the difference.[8]

Persecution Brings Reward

Jesus Christ does *not* say, "Happy are those who make a nuisance of themselves. Happy are the lazy, the unethical, the sloppy, the irritating, and the arrogant."

No, Jesus Christ says, "Happy are those who are harassed *because* of godly living."

The apostle Peter writes along these same lines;

Beloved, do not be surprised at the fiery trial when it comes upon you to test you, as though something strange were happening to you. But rejoice insofar as you share Christ's sufferings, that you may also rejoice and be glad when his glory is revealed (I Peter 4:12-13).

This is the promised reward of the kingdom and the reward in heaven in Matthew 5.

Peter continues:

If you are insulted for the name of Christ, you are blessed [*makarios*, which is the same word Christ used in His sermon, meaning "you are truly happy"], *because the Spirit of glory and of God rests upon you. But let none of you suffer as a murderer or a thief or an evildoer or as a meddler. Yet if anyone suffers as a Christian, let him not be ashamed, but let him glorify God in that name* [that is, in the name "Christian"] (I Peter 4:14-16).

Notice also that Jesus Christ did *not* say, "Happy are those who are persecuted—period." He said, "Happy are those who are persecuted for righteousness." In other words, He was saying, "You can be truly happy as you share in suffering because you know your reward one day will be great."

People around the world are making a decision to suffer for Christ when they choose the name *Christian*.

Fourteen former Muslims in Morocco made the conscious decision to identify with Christ as their Lord and Master. After the baptism of these fourteen converts in a secret cove along the water's edge, suddenly an observer leaped into the water, tears in his eyes, and declared he, too, wanted to be a follower of Christ and be baptized. The man—a Muslim himself—had been the interpreter for the training meetings that week. Before being baptized, he had to answer publicly the questions the others had answered before they were immersed:

- Do you renounce Islam, the Koran, Ramadan, and other teachings of the Muslim faith?
- Have you accepted Christ as your Lord and Savior, and do you now believe in the Trinity—that Christ is equally God?
- Are you willing to be imprisoned; to be thrown out of your home for Christ?

Upon his positive response, he was baptized a follower of Jesus Christ.

Imagine the depth of their decision to identify with Christ. But no matter what happens to these fifteen, they know that they have found true, abiding happiness.

Jesus ended this beatitude by saying, "Rejoice and be glad, for your reward in heaven is great!"

Wow—happiness . . . and heaven, too!

Happiness . . . and Heaven, Too

All of Christ's statements in Matthew 5 have spelled out true happiness, in contrast to the world's vain pursuit:

- *verse 3:* "Blessed are those who recognize they are spiritually poverty stricken."

    the world: "Happy are those who don't need anything . . . or anyone."

- *verse 4:* "Happy are those who mourn over their sinful desires."

    the world: "Happy are those who never have to confess to anything."

- ***verse 5:*** "Happy are those who refuse to retaliate."

  the world: "Happy are those who climb over anyone in their way."
- ***verse 6:*** "Happy are those who are starving for the things of God."

  the world: "Happy are those with a garage full of toys."
- ***verse 7:*** "Happy are those who lend a hand to help others."

  the world: "You've gotta be kidding—happiness is when you're served 24/7."
- ***verse 8:*** "Happy are those whose private purity is a daily resolution."

  the world: "Happiness is when your private impurity never makes it into the newspaper!"
- ***verse 9***: "Happy are those who negotiate peace."

  the world: "Happy are those who fight their way to the top."
- ***verses 10 & 11:*** "Happy are those who are harassed for My sake."

  the world: "Happy are the trouble-free."

Cassius Clay [*aka* Muhammad Ali] was the former three-time world heavyweight boxing champion—the Tiger Woods of boxing in his day. No one could match his skill in the ring for years.

Ali's face was on *Sports Illustrated* more times than any other athlete in its history. When he was "floating like a butterfly, stinging like a bee," he was on top of his profession and everyone knew it.

Sports reporter Gary Smith was invited to his estate to tour the grounds long after Ali hung up his gloves. Ali took him into a refurnished barn which was located at the back of the property. It had been converted to showcase all of Ali's memorabilia and was filled from floor to ceiling with pictures, articles, plaques, and trophies.

On one wall there were a number of magazine covers displaying his picture. The covers had been enlarged to life-size photographs, and framed in glass. As the reporter stood gaping in amazement, Ali walked over to the frames and peered at them. He was perturbed by the traces of droppings from the birds who still made their home in the barn and had no respect for their legendary host.

After mumbling something under his breath, Ali shuffled to the doorway of the barn and stood staring out into space. Gary said, "Excuse me, what did you say?"

Ali repeated louder, this time not just to himself, "I was saying, 'I had the world—and it was nothin' . . . it was nothin.'"

Imagine coming to that reality late in life . . . "I had the world . . . and it was nothing."

How right he was!

I can't help but think of what Jesus Christ is saying to us right now. He's speaking to those of us who rarely make headlines; we're often trodden underfoot and sometimes overlooked: "You may not have the world *now*, but you *will* one day. In fact, you'll have a *new* world—and it will be *something*."

Just hearing that promise from Jesus Christ brings an abiding sense of happiness, even in the face of persecution . . . no matter what may come.

So let it come. One day you will have the world, my friend—and it will be something. *Wow,* will it be something!

We have happiness now, but happiness and heaven . . . *forever!*

Scripture Index

Reference	Page	Reference	Page
Romans 3:21-22	46	Galatians 6:1	45
Romans 3:23-24	62	Ephesians 2:4	56
Romans 5:1	69	Colossians 1:19-20	69
Romans 7:18	14	II Timothy 1:3b-4a	27
Romans 8:22	26	Titus 3:5	56
Romans 15:4	36	Hebrews 11:13, 16	21
Romans 15:13	36	James 1:21	44
I Corinthians 3:21-23a	43	James 5:11	19
II Corinthians 1:3	35	I Peter 3:15-17	44
II Corinthians 1:4	37	I Peter 4:12-13	74
II Corinthians 2:4	28	I Peter 4:14-16	75
II Corinthians 5:9	47	I John 1:7	32
II Corinthians 5:20	70	I John 3:17	57
II Corinthians 7:10	31	Revelation 1:3	20
Galatians 5:22-23	46	Revelation 21:4	37

Endnotes

Chapter 1

[1] John MacArthur, *Kingdom Living Here and Now* (Moody Press, 1980), p. 26.
[2] Fritz Rienecker and Cleon Rogers, *Linguistic Key to the Greek New Testament* (Regency, 1976), p. 12.
[3] *Ibid.*, p. 22.
[4] Robert J. Morgan, *Thomas Nelson's Complete Book of Stories* (Thomas Nelson, 2000), p. 406.
[5] Scott Wenig, #182, http://wwwpreachingtoday.com.
[6] MacArthur, p. 37.
[7] Rienecker and Rogers, p. 12.
[8] R. Kent Hughes, *The Sermon on the Mount* (Crossway, 2001), p. 19.
[9] Thomas Watson, *The Beatitudes* (Banner of Truth, 1985 ed. of 1660 ed.), p. 42.
[10] MacArthur, p. 45.
[11] Watson, p. 46.
[12] MacArthur, p. 49.
[13] *Ibid.*, p. 50.
[14] Hughes, p. 21.
[15] Warren Wiersbe, *Live Like a King* (Moody, 1976), p. 22.
[16] John Calvin, *Sermons on the Beatitudes* translated by Robert White (Banner of Truth Trust, 2006 ed. of 1560 ed.).
[17] Joni Eareckson Tada, "Joy Hard-Won," *Decision* (Mar. 2000), p. 12.

Chapter 2

[1] John MacArthur, *Kingdom Living* (Moody Press, 1980), p. 55.
[2] Warren Wiersbe, *Living Like a King* (Moody Press, 1975), p. 45.
[3] Thomas Watson, *The Beatitudes* (Banner of Truth Trust, 1985 ed. of 1660 ed.), p. 59.
[4] R. Kent Hughes, *The Sermon on the Mount* (Crossway Books, 2001), p. 26.
[5] Fritz Rienecker and Cleon Rogers, *Linguistic Key to the Greek New Testament* (Regency, 1976), p. 785.
[6] William Cowper, "There Is a Fountain," *Praise Hymnal*.
[7] MacArthur, p. 61.
[8] Wiersbe, p. 56.

Chapter 3

[1] R. Kent Hughes, *The Sermon on the Mount* (Crossway Books, 2001), p. 33.

[2] Matthew Henry, *The Quest for Meekness and Quietness of Spirit* (Soli Deo Gloria Publications, 1996 ed. of 1698 ed.), p. 34.

[3] John MacArthur, *Kingdom Living Here and Now* (Moody Press, 1980), p. 77.

[4] Michael Hodgin, *1001 Humorous Illustrations* (Zondervan Publishing, 1994), p. 96.

[5] Warren Wiersbe, *Live Like a King* (Moody Press, 1976), p. 63.

[6] Ibid., p. 64.

[7] MacArthur, p. 85.

[8] Ibid., p. 77.

[9] Hughes, p. 40.

[10] *Heartcry!*, Issue 26 (2003).

[11] MacArthur, p. 100.

Chapter 4

[1] John MacArthur, *Kingdom Living Here and Now* (Moody Press, 1980), p. 105.

[2] Warren Wiersbe, *Live Like a King* (Moody Press, 1976), p. 105.

[3] R. Kent Hughes, *The Sermon on the Mount* (Crossway Books, 2001), p. 48.

[4] Wiersbe, p. 95.

[5] MacArthur, p. 109.

[6] Hughes, p. 46.

[7] James Montgomery Boice, *The Sermon on the Mount* (Baker Books, 1972), p. 46.

[8] MacArthur, p. 133.

[9] Wiersbe, p. 122.

[10] Hughes, p. 56.

Chapter 5

[1] Charles Swindoll, *Job: Man of Heroic Endurance* (W Publishing, 2004), p. 98.

[2] R. Kent Hughes, *The Sermon On the Mount* (Crossway Books, 2001), p. 62.

[3] John MacArthur, *Kingdom Living Here and Now* (Moody Press, 1980), p. 129.

[4] Warren Wiersbe, *Live Like a King* (Moody Press, 1976), p. 129.

[5] Hughes, p. 64.

[6] Robert L. Peterson and Alexander Strauch, *Agape Leadership* (Lewis & Roth Publishers, 1991), p. 44.

[7] MacArthur, p. 159.

[8] Wiersbe, p. 138.